W9-COX-492

THE ST LAWRENCE

Julia Waterlow

photographed by Laurence Fordyce

Wayland

THE WORLD'S RIVERS

The Amazon
The Danube
The Ganges
The Mississippi
The Nile
The Rhine
The St Lawrence
The Seine
The Thames
The Volga
The Yellow River
The Zaire

Cover The mighty St Lawrence seen from Québec city.

Series editor Rosemary Ashley
Series designer Derek Lee
Book designer Paul Bennett

First published in 1994 by
Wayland (Publishers) Limited
61 Western Road, Hove
East Sussex, BN3 1JD, England

© Copyright 1994
Wayland (Publishers) Limited

British Library Cataloguing in Publication Data
Waterlow, Julia
St Lawrence River.—(World's Rivers Series)
I. Title II. Series
917.14

ISBN 0-7502-1259-4

Typeset in the UK by
Dorchester Typesetting Group Ltd
Printed in Italy by G. Canale C.S.p.A.
Bound in France by AGM

CONTENTS

1. INTO THE HEART OF A CONTINENT

The St Lawrence River flows from the heart of North America into the Atlantic Ocean. From the sea the river provides a route for ships to take people and goods right into the centre of the continent. Over the last three hundred and fifty years this waterway has been vitally important in opening up and developing the interior of North America, in particular Canada.

The St Lawrence is fed by the waters of the Great Lakes of North America, five huge lakes, almost like seas, that together contain one-fifth of the world's surface fresh water. By following the St Lawrence upstream and then travelling across these lakes, ocean-going ships can now reach 3,750 km inland. This has been possible only in the last thirty-five years, with the building of the St Lawrence Seaway; early explorers of the continent were faced with rapids and waterfalls that barred their way. Canals and locks now allow ships to bypass these hazards.

Canada and the United States share a border along part of the river and through the Great Lakes. During the past four hundred years, millions of Europeans and people from other continents have come to settle in these countries. Because of the many natural resources in the region around the St Lawrence and the Great Lakes, this area has become densely inhabited and developed. Today it is one of the most heavily populated and industrialized areas of the North American continent, if not of the world. As a result there are many pressures on the St Lawrence and the Great Lakes. They are needed as transport highways, for their water to supply factories and houses, for leisure and sport and as a home for the natural wildlife of the region; they are also used as a dumping-ground for human waste.

In its lower reaches, the St Lawrence River widens to more than thirty kilometres across.

4

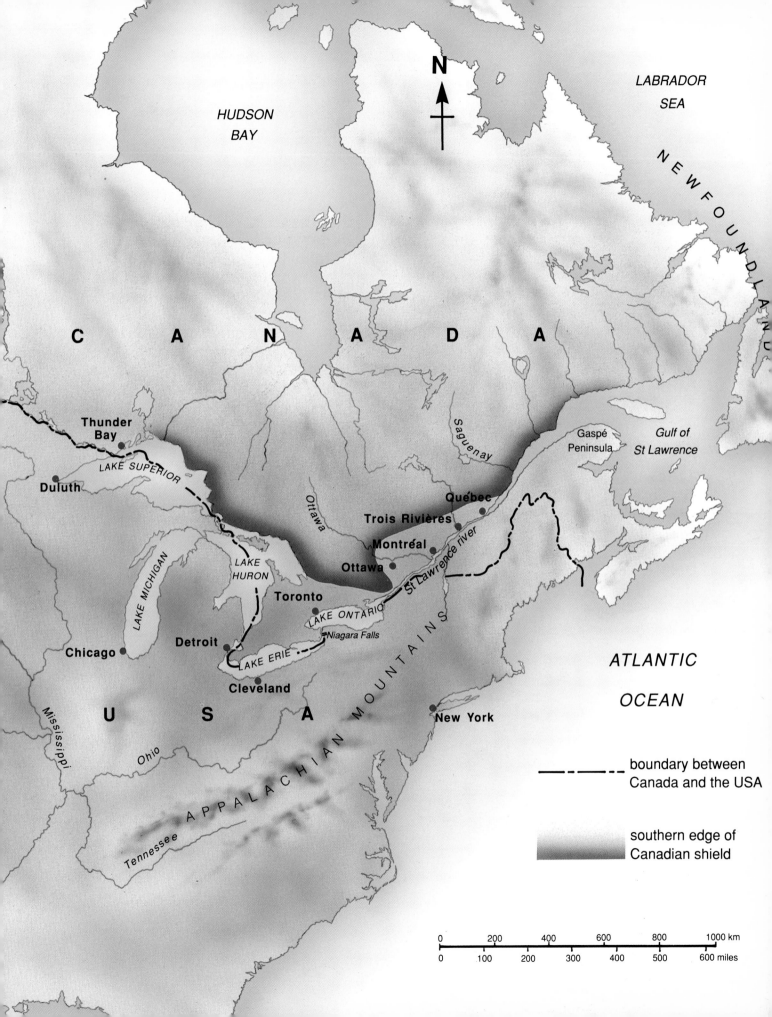

N

HUDSON
BAY

LABRADOR
SEA

NEWFOUNDLAND

C   A   N   A   D   A

Thunder
Bay

Saguenay

Gaspé
Peninsula

Gulf of
St Lawrence

LAKE SUPERIOR

Duluth

Ottawa

Québec

Trois Rivières

Montréal

LAKE
HURON

LAKE
MICHIGAN

Ottawa

St Lawrence river

Toronto

ATLANTIC

OCEAN

LAKE ONTARIO

Detroit

Niagara Falls

Chicago

LAKE ERIE

U   S   A

Cleveland

New York

Mississippi

Ohio

A P P A L A C H I A N   M O U N T A I N S

Tennessee

boundary between
Canada and the USA

southern edge of
Canadian shield

0	200	400	600	800	1000 km
0	100	200	300	400	500	600 miles

2. THE RIVER AND THE LAND

The course of the river

Unlike most great rivers, the St Lawrence does not start as a small stream high up in mountains but begins as a large river pouring out of the great dish of water formed by the five Great Lakes. The official beginning is where the river flows out of Lake Ontario; here it is about 75 m above sea-level and has about 1,300 km to travel north-east before it reaches its mouth in the Gulf of St Lawrence.

On the first stretch of its journey, the St Lawrence splits into numerous channels that wind around pretty islands. The area is called the Thousand Islands (although there are actually nearer two thousand). All along this section of the river upstream of the city of Montréal, rapids used to make travel difficult and foiled early explorers. As it reaches Montréal, the St Lawrence is joined by the Ottawa River, one of its hundred or so tributaries.

Still hundreds of kilometres from the

Thousands of islands dot the St Lawrence as it begins its journey from the Great Lakes, in the area known as The Thousand Islands.

This bridge at Trois Rivières is one of the few road bridges spanning the St Lawrence downstream of Montréal.

sea, near the town of Trois Rivières, the St Lawrence becomes tidal (this means that the effects of the daily sea tides can be seen and the river rises and falls). Only a little further downstream, the river broadens out. From just 1.5 km across where it passes the city of Québec, the St Lawrence spreads so wide that it is often difficult to see to the far side.

The river banks become steep and wild; the deep Saguenay River joins the St Lawrence. Gradually the river widens out into the Gulf of St Lawrence. The Percé Rock that juts out of the sea at the end of the Gaspé peninsula stands marking the river's finish. The area is wild and windswept with cliffs, beaches and coves. Beyond, the gaping mouth of the Gulf of St Lawrence opens out towards the Atlantic Ocean with the rocky island of Newfoundland like a giant tooth in the middle.

A cross-section of the Great Lakes and St Lawrence from Lake Superior to the Atlantic.

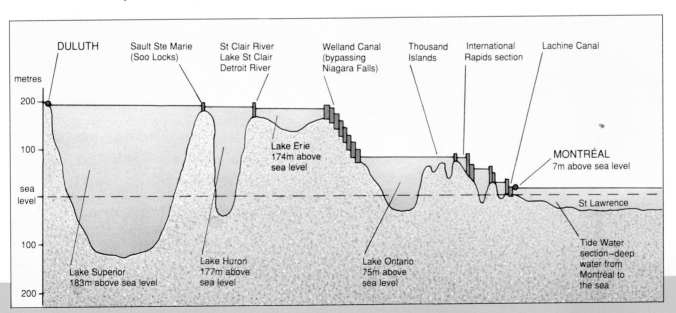

7

The Percé Rock stands at the top of the Gaspé Peninsula with its cliffs and coves. Here the St Lawrence flows out into the Gulf of St Lawrence.

The Great Lakes

The St Lawrence River and the Great Lakes that feed it have always been important to each other. The two have become even more interlinked since the St Lawrence Seaway was built, making a navigable waterway for large ships. The Great Lakes have the largest surface of fresh water in the world: the biggest, Lake Superior, is over 550 km long and covers an area twice the size of Switzerland. Except for Lake Erie, the lakes are all very deep, the bottom being well below sea-level (see the diagram on page 7).

Each lake has some kind of barrier at its outlet, whether it be a narrow channel, rapids or a waterfall over which water from one lake flows into the next. The greatest drop in level is between Lake Erie and Lake Ontario, where water flows out along the Niagara River, rushing over many rapids. It then suddenly pours over a ridge of rock, the famous Niagara Falls, dropping some 60 metres before flowing into Lake Ontario.

Ice action

It took powerful forces of nature to create the huge water-filled basins that we call the Great Lakes. They were formed during the last Ice Age that lasted many thousands of years. Ice from the North Pole spread south in a great sheet across North America. The furthest it reached was just south of where the Great Lakes now lie.

Ice is very hard and as it moves, it can crush and grind rock. In North America, over thousands of years, ice gouged deep basins where the rock was particularly soft. When the climate warmed and the ice retreated (the ice finally disappeared from North America about ten thousand years ago), great bodies of meltwater from the ice were left. At the same time the land was very slowly beginning to rise. The sea of meltwater from the ice spilt out along a fault in the rock, forming a river, the St Lawrence. The Great Lakes were left behind in their deep basins.

These are the Horseshoe Falls, the most dramatic section of the famous Niagara Falls.

Vast areas of forest stretch across the Canadian Shield to the north of the St Lawrence.

Landscape and climate

The St Lawrence River lies sandwiched between the Appalachian Mountains to its south and the Canadian Shield that stretches across most of northern Canada up towards Hudson Bay. The Canadian Shield is an area of very hard and old rock that was so scoured and eroded by ice during the Ice Age that it is almost bare of soil in many places and is pock-marked by thousands of small lakes. As well as swampy areas called *muskeg*, there are also forests.

The Canadian Shield reaches down to the edge of the St Lawrence along most of its north bank. The St Lawrence lowlands, with the best farming land in Canada and home to most Canadian people and their cities, lie in a narrow strip by the river in the province of Québec. This strip widens out as the river nears Lake Ontario.

Unlike the hard rock of the Canadian Shield that was scraped by ice, in the Great Lakes region, on the edge of the ice sheet, silt and soil were dropped. This rich layer made it easier for plants to grow and the area was once heavily forested. It now makes good farming land.

The climate of the region has a great effect on how the land is used and how the people live. Winters are severe, with biting Arctic winds bringing icy temperatures that freeze the upper reaches of the St Lawrence for months. Every year there is heavy snowfall.

Right *Farmland in Québec lies in strips down to the river. This pattern was laid out by early settlers, giving each homestead access to the river.*

Below *Winter can be bitterly cold. Here, Lake Ontario is frozen, with ice up to half a metre thick.*

Despite this, summers are hot enough for people to enjoy swimming in the lakes and rivers.

Weather around the Great Lakes is affected by the lakes themselves; they are so large that they alter the temperature in the same way as the sea does, keeping the area warmer than normal in winter. This is because water does not cool down as quickly as land and it retains some of the summer's warmth. Even so, the temperatures of the lakes still fall below zero in winter and snow falls in thick blankets.

Facts and figures
Length of river: 1,290 km
Distance from Lake Ontario to Atlantic Ocean at Cabot Strait: about 2,000 km.
Names of lakes: Superior, Michigan, Huron, Erie and Ontario. Only Michigan is totally within the United States, the others share their boundaries with Canada.
Area drained by Great Lakes and St Lawrence River: 1,760,000 sq km (3 times the size of France).
Size of Great Lakes: inland sea of 245,000 sq km (the same size as the whole area of Great Britain).

3. OPENING UP THE INTERIOR

The first settlers

During the last Ice Age temperatures were so low that the sea froze, making a bridge between Siberia (in Asia) and Alaska (the most north-westerly point of America). About thirty thousand years ago people from Asia first started migrating into and across the Americas. Most were hunters and nomads.

These native Americans, or Indians, as they came to be called by Europeans, grouped themselves into tribes. They lived in different parts of the continent, each having their own culture and beliefs. Some relied on fishing; others hunted animals. For example, those who settled on the wide open plains called prairies, west of the Great Lakes, were buffalo hunters.

The area around the St Lawrence and Great Lakes was home to many tribes, some of whom settled down and grew crops in the river valley. This way of life remained unaltered for centuries until the arrival of Europeans.

A sixteenth-century map showing Jacques Cartier landing in Canada. It was drawn the opposite way to today's maps – the big island on the left is Newfoundland.

An old painting of a trading post run by the Hudson's Bay Company shows beaver furs being bundled up ready for transporting.

New arrivals

In 1535 Jacques Cartier, a Frenchman, sailed up the St Lawrence River as far as where Montréal lies today. He could travel no further because his way was blocked by rapids. Like John Cabot, who had visited the east coast of Canada in 1497, Cartier had been searching for a route to China. Instead he discovered the gateway into a new continent.

Following in his footsteps came French adventurers and merchants. They found a wild and untamed country, and they discovered the beaver. Its pelts of soft fur were taken to Europe where beaver soon became fashionable (especially for hats).

The St Lawrence was the easiest way to travel into the heart of the new country (soon to be called New France) because the land all around was forest and rugged terrain. And so it was on the banks of the St Lawrence that a capital, Québec, was founded in 1608 by Samuel de Champlain. Not long after, settlers arrived and began to farm.

The British too were exploring parts of Canada, but to the north around Hudson Bay. Traders from both Britain and France set up fur companies, of which the best known was the Hudson's Bay Company. This British company eventually controlled vast areas of northern Canada.

13

The native North Americans were one source of supply of furs; many gave up their traditional way of life to become fur trappers for the Europeans. As the demand for furs continued, traders went deeper and deeper into the unexplored heart of Canada. Trading posts were set up along their routes, especially beside the navigable rivers and on the shores of the Great Lakes.

The British and the French were rivals, both in Europe and in North America. War broke out between them and the British decided to attack the French settlements along the

The Hudson's Bay Company

Until 1870 the huge northern area around Hudson Bay was not part of Canada. Instead it was controlled by the Hudson's Bay Company. This was a British fur company that caught and shipped beaver furs to Europe via Hudson Bay, without using the French-controlled St Lawrence River. Explorers and adventurers working for the company pushed deep into the interior searching for new areas to find beavers. The fur trappers mostly did not settle – at the beginning of Canada's history people farmed and built towns only along the narrow strip by the banks of the St Lawrence.

A fur trapper in the nineteenth century struggles through the icy wilderness of Canada.

St Lawrence. Québec was the largest town and so the main target. In a famous battle in the year 1759, General Wolfe successfully led the British in an assault on the Plains of Abraham (the hill on which the French fort lay). In 1763 the French admitted defeat and their Canadian territories were given to Britain. British settlers joined the French along the shores of the St Lawrence and established new settlements beside the Great Lakes.

Not long after, to the south, war broke out between Britain and its American colonies (the American War of Independence) because the Americans no longer wanted to be ruled by a country far away across the Atlantic. Settlers in Canada however did not join in and remained loyal to the British crown. After Independence in 1783, America continued to argue with Britain about control of land around the Great Lakes. War broke out in 1812. When the Americans tried to capture Montréal and Québec, British and French Canadian settlers fought side by side to defeat the Americans. It was not until many years later that the border between the two countries was finally agreed.

In 1867 Canada formed its own government, independent of Britain, with a new capital at Ottawa. During the 1870s the Canadian Pacific Railway opened up the west of Canada to settlers and people streamed across the country. However, the St Lawrence valley remained the heartland of Canada and it was here that the increasing population and industrial growth of the next century was to take place.

Above *This French fort guarded the mouth of the Niagara River on Lake Ontario.*

Right *The Parliament buildings in Ottawa, Canada's capital.*

4. PEOPLE OF THE ST LAWRENCE

Students biking for charity – the sign on their giant cycle is in French and English, the two languages of Canada.

There is probably nowhere else on earth with such a mixture of races living together, and relatively peacefully. The largest group, about half, is of British origin and about a quarter of the people are French, but there are also Germans, Ukranians, Italians, Dutch, Scandinavians, Polish, Chinese and others from many countries. Between one and two per cent of the population are native North Americans. Most Canadians are proud of their European and other roots and their country that is home for people from all over the world.

Native Canadians

Native North Americans lived and farmed the land around the St Lawrence and Great Lakes long before the arrival of the Europeans. The Huron tribe were one group who settled in what came to be called Ontario, growing corn and tobacco. They would trade with other tribes such as the Algonquins, who lived a nomadic life in the forests to the north-west of the St Lawrence and hunted moose and deer and caught fish. Often the Hurons fought members of the Iroquois Confederacy. These were a

16

Right *Native Canadians at a modern Pow Wow (gathering).*

Left *A native Canadian member of the Algonquin tribe, from the region north-west of the St Lawrence, strips corn cobs into a cooking pot.*

Dwight Teeple

'I was born in a log cabin at the Bay Mills Indian Community. When I was small we had no electricity and carried our water from a well half a mile away. I belong to the Chippewa tribe which is part of a large language group including many other tribes such as the Ottawa, Blackfoot, Shawnee, Illinois and so on. Some folk think that if we believe in the old ways we should go back to doing things in the old way – for example, living in a teepee or fishing for food. I don't agree with this. We are continually adapting to the new technologies available to us. I have always felt it a challenge to be a native Canadian.'

ferocious group of five tribes who also lived in this area and included the Mohawks. West of the Great Lakes were the buffalo-hunting tribes of the prairies; until Spanish explorers brought horses to the Americas, they hunted on foot.

The arrival of Europeans changed the lives of the native tribes of Canada for ever. Many abandoned their traditional hunting lifestyles in order to trap furs to trade with Europeans. From the white people they bought food and guns and gradually they became dependent on the Europeans for survival. Thousands of native Americans died from European diseases to which they had no resistance. Fighting broke out too between the tribes as they fought each other for control of the fur trade.

On the prairies, the tribes were nearly wiped out not only by disease but by the introduction of the gun. This led to overhunting of the buffalo which was their livelihood. As settlers spread across Canada, the tribes surrendered their lands to the Canadian government. From a population of about one million, by 1867 the number of native North Americans in Canada had dropped to 112,000.

In the 1920s the numbers began to increase again and, although most native Canadians now live in cities, some have returned to their traditional lifestyles, hunting and fishing for their food. They have had to persuade the government to give them back land so that they can live in protected reservations of their own.

The French question

The French were the first Europeans to settle along the St Lawrence River and they kept their language and traditions even after Britain took over Canada. But it was not long before there were more British than French living there and the numbers swelled when Loyalists

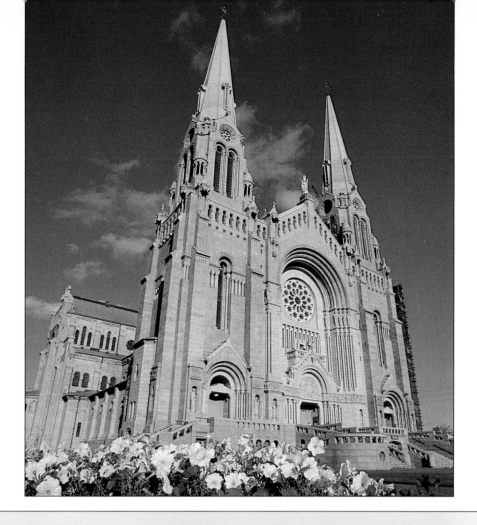

The church of St Anne de Beaupré is a French Catholic shrine. Thousands of visitors come to it every year.

Nichole Deschènes Duval

'I am a sculptor, working in Québec City. I am a French Canadian and I believe that the province of Québec should be an independent country with its own government. We French Canadians feel almost as if we are a conquered people – conquered by the English-speaking rest of Canada. All the other French Canadians, and those in parts of the USA too, have been absorbed into English-speaking communities, losing their language and their culture. I believe that we in Québec are the only hope for a French civilization in North America. We just want our independence from English Canada. We are not a movement against anyone, we only want to preserve our culture.'

Chinatown in Toronto. Many Chinese have come to settle in Canada.

(Americans who remained loyal to the British crown when others fought for American independence from Britain) poured into Canada after the American War of Independence.

The French Canadians however were still the majority in the cities of Montréal and Québec in the province of Québec. Even today Montréal is the second largest French-speaking city in the world, after Paris. In the 1960s there was a movement by the French Canadians to make Québec province independent of the rest of Canada because they felt their culture, language and history were so different. A political party came to power that, among other laws, made French the official language in Québec.

Canada is now bilingual, that is both English and French are official languages and are taught in all the schools. However, many French Canadians want Québec province to have self-rule, with its own government in Québec city. Although it is unlikely Canada's government will accept that Québec should be independent, the importance of French culture is recognized.

Immigration

Canada, like the United States, has been the destination for one of the greatest movements of people the world has ever seen. In 1800 Canada's population was little more than half a million; in the early 1900s some two million people arrived from abroad and since then there have been another six or seven million immigrants.

Most people came from Europe, leaving as a result of poverty, persecution, homelessness after war, and unemployment in their own countries. For example, Scandinavians came in the 1860s to work as lumberjacks in the forests around the Great Lakes. In the early 1900s the Canadian government encouraged people to come to Canada to help settle the prairies in the west. After the end of the Second World War (in 1945) there was a great flood of people from Europe searching for a new home and new life. In recent years, more and more immigrants have been arriving from Asia. Today between 100,000 and 200,000 newcomers arrive in Canada each year.

5. SETTLEMENTS

The native Canadians never built towns. Most of them were nomadic although some settled in villages near the St Lawrence. With the coming of the Europeans all this changed and towns and cities grew where there was previously wild and uninhabited land. Today the majority of Canadians live in towns and cities.

The first settlements were beside the St Lawrence River where ships from Europe could dock, bringing people and supplies and taking back furs. Farms grew up in a line along the waterfront because the river was the early settlers' road. It provided plenty of fish for food and, because the land close to the river had less trees, it was easier to farm.

A view over Québec from the cliffs above the St Lawrence. On the left is Chateau Frontenac, a famous landmark.

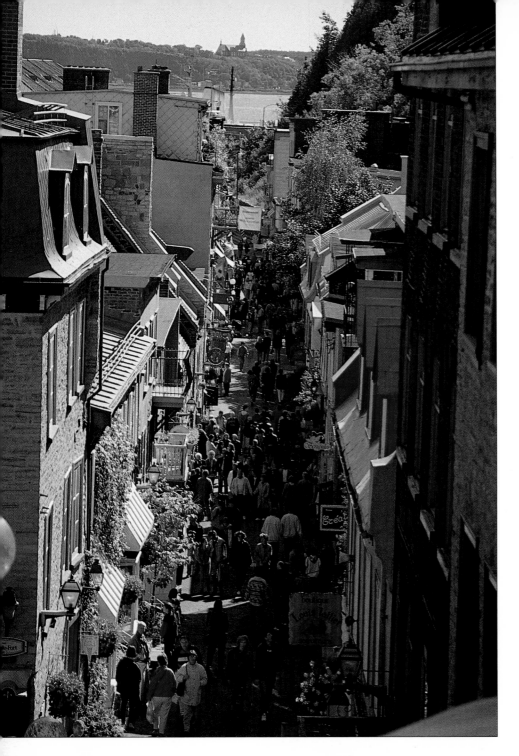

Rue Petit Champlain in the old quarter of Québec preserves the charm of a French city.

The French cities – Québec and Montréal

The city of Québec was the first city to be founded along the St Lawrence. It lies at the point where the river narrows (the name comes from a native word *kebec* meaning 'place where the water narrows'). Cliffs rise up steeply from the river and so it was a natural place for Samuel de Champlain to build a fort to defend the French traders and settlers. Many of the city's old buildings have been kept and preserved. Because the majority of people here speak French and are proud of their French roots and culture, the city feels very much like a town in France.

Although Québec was the capital of New France for a time, the city of Montréal gradually took over in importance. Founded in 1642, the settlement grew up along the wooded slopes of Mont Royale on an island where the Ottawa River joins the St Lawrence. This was an important meeting point of routes for the traders in the early days. Although originally French, the city has become a mix of French and English as well as being home to many other nationalities.

Today Montréal is the second most important city in Canada. It is a major business centre and lies in the middle of a large manufacturing region. Its huge docks along the river handle thousands of tonnes of cargo every year. Modern skyscrapers rise up above ground, while far below is an underground maze of shops, restaurants and offices linked by the underground railway, the Metro. During the freezing winters, the people of Montréal can spend their time warm inside their underground city.

Tall skyscrapers rise up in the heart of Montréal close to docks on the St Lawrence.

Cities of the Great Lakes

Toronto lies on the northern shore of Lake Ontario, an English-speaking city established by the Loyalists who left America after Independence. It is the largest as well as the most important city in Canada. Full of gleaming modern buildings, Toronto is a lively place where people enjoy arts, music and other entertainment. Around the cultural and commercial centre are a huge number of different manufacturing industries. Together with Montréal, Toronto forms the industrial heartland of Canada.

Like many North American cities, Toronto has grown so rapidly that there is severe traffic congestion in the central area. It is difficult finding a solution for cities like this; in Toronto, offices have been built in landscaped parks on the edge of the city to ease traffic problems in the centre. Other cities beside the Great Lakes suffer from congestion and overcrowding too. The built-up areas of the lakeside towns have spread many kilometres, and in places towns just merge one into another along the shores.

The largest lakeside cities are Chicago, Detroit and Cleveland, all of which lie in the United States. Chicago,

The modern city of Toronto with its tall landmark, the CN tower, sprawls alongside Lake Ontario.

sometimes called the 'Windy City', was home to less than a hundred people in 1830 but is now one of the largest cities in North America. It grew when the railroad was built across the United States, making it a point where goods could be transferred between ships on Lake Michigan and the railway. Factories producing iron and steel were set up here because bulky raw materials (iron and coal) could be brought in easily by ship and the products sent to markets all over the United States by rail. As well as being a centre for heavy industry, Chicago is also an important grain market for the wheat producing areas of the United States's Midwest.

Detroit began, like Chicago, as a fur-trading town at a crossing point on the Great Lakes route. Now, factories in the city manufacture all sorts of products but Detroit is most famous for its car industry and is headquarters for world-famous companies such as Ford, Chrysler and General Motors. Cleveland, like several other U.S. cities on Lake Erie, is a major iron and steel producing centre.

The city of Detroit is typical of some of the huge industrial cities that lie on the Great Lakes.

6. FARMING AND INDUSTRY

A large modern dairy farm near Lake Michigan supplies the cities of the Great Lakes area.

Farming and fishing

On the northern side of the St Lawrence valley the rugged Canadian Shield comes down to the edge of the river. For holidaymakers who enjoy the hilly scenery for walking, skiing or hunting this is fine, but it is not easy land to farm. Most farms lie to the south-east of the river where the land is flatter and the soil better. This area, together with land around lakes Ontario and Erie, is the most intensively farmed part of Canada.

Farmers mainly raise dairy cows, supplying the big cities of the St Lawrence with milk, butter and cheese. Around lakes Ontario and Erie is an area called the Niagara Fruit Belt: because of the milder climate due to the lakes, fruits such as apples, cherries and peaches grow well. There are even vineyards. Market gardening is important too to provide the cities with fresh vegetables. The St Lawrence and Great Lakes region is a productive farming area, first because it has the longest growing season in Canada

Wheat farming

The prairies of western Canada are one of the most important farming areas in the developed world – each farmer produces enough grain and meat to feed fifty five people for a year. About 98 per cent of Canada's wheat comes from here. The farms use huge machines that can efficiently harvest the wide flat open land. Because the summers are so short and there can be times without any rain, special wheat types are used that grow quickly and can survive with little water.

A farm on the Ile d'Orleans in the St Lawrence River; the houses have steep-pitched roofs so that the snow slides off easily in winter.

Left *Fruit grown in the area known as the Niagara Fruit Belt.*

Right *Vineyards near Lake Ontario.*

(the warming effect of the Great Lakes) and second it has fertile soils left by the retreating ice thousands of years ago.

Dairy farming continues alongside the other Great Lakes but further to the west the land gives way to the prairies. These vast open plains stretching 1,700 km from east to west are covered in glacial silt left by the ice and are naturally fertile. Originally the prairies were grasslands, but European settlers ploughed up the land and started to grow wheat. Today the prairies of North America are sometimes called the 'breadbasket of the world' because they produce so much wheat.

Good fishing grounds lie near the mouth of the St Lawrence. Before they explored the land and started hunting beaver, Europeans discovered that these rich waters were teeming with fish such as cod. The shores of Newfoundland until recently were some of the most productive cod fishing grounds in the world. However, there has been so much overfishing that in order to stop the fish from being completely wiped out, the government has brought in fish 'quotas'. These allow fishermen to catch only a certain amount of fish every year. Today the most valuable fishing catch near the mouth of the St Lawrence is lobster.

Cod fish are dried on racks out in the open on the Gaspé Peninsula.

Resources and industry

The St Lawrence area, like much of Canada, has many useful natural resources, such as the forests that grow on the Canadian Shield and around the St Lawrence and the Great Lakes. The trees are cut, floated down rivers and pulped at paper mills. Mills, such as those at Trois Rivières, Baie-Comeau and Chicoutimi-Jonquière, lie beside rivers because ships are the easiest way to transport bulky timber products (paper and pulp). The rivers too provide hydroelectricity which is a convenient source of power for the timber mills. Although in the past the land was stripped of its trees without any thought for replanting, forestry in Canada is now carefully managed; trees are treated as a crop that has to be harvested and replanted.

Forestry
The Canadians realize the forests are an important resource that must be carefully looked after. Trees used to be chopped down and nothing was put back, but now many are replanted. The timber industry relies on heavy machinery: the trees are felled with chainsaws and large vehicles drag or lift them into piles. Lakes and rivers are still used for transport by tying the trees together in log rafts and towing them downriver. Wood pulp and paper are Canada's second most important export.

The Canadian Shield is one of the richest mineral areas in the world with reserves of iron, silver, platinum, gold, copper, nickel, zinc and uranium. Mining is a difficult process because of the severe climate and problems of reaching remote areas where many of the minerals are found. One such place is the large iron ore mine of Schefferville (this is shown on the map on page 37). A 600 km-long railway was built to connect the mine with the port of Sept-Iles which lies on the St Lawrence, the nearest convenient route for transporting the iron ore.

The lowland region of the St Lawrence is Canada's main manufacturing centre; around Montréal and Toronto factories produce everything from vehicles, chemicals and hi-tech electrical products to furniture and drinks. Industries like these, as well as timber and mining, need a great deal of power. Canada uses its thousands of rivers to produce hydroelectricity; by damming the rivers the water flow is controlled and its power used to make electricity. The tributaries of the St Lawrence such as the Ottawa and Saguenay Rivers have the largest

A steel mill at Sault Ste Marie. The iron ore and coal it uses are brought by ship across the Great Lakes.

This bridge is made out of the metal aluminium. Nearby is the huge aluminium plant at Chicoutimi-Jonquière on the Saguenay River, a tributary of the St Lawrence.

hydroelectric stations but the rapids and waterfalls on the St Lawrence itself are also harnessed to make electrical power.

One of the important hydroelectric plants is at Niagara Falls. To produce electricity, water has to be diverted from the falls to the hydroelectric station; but because they are such a famous tourist sight, water can only be diverted at night. Industries that need large supplies of power have been attracted here, for example chemical and aluminium manufacturers. The short Niagara River is lined with industrial buildings and has become a 'chemical valley', full of factories.

Aluminium is produced at Chicoutimi-Jonquière on the Saguenay River, where there is plenty of cheap hydroelectricity. Aluminium ore is brought from abroad to be processed in Canada; the deep Saguenay tributary of the St Lawrence allows large ships far upstream.

Canada has so much hydroelectric power that it sells its surplus to the United States. Although hydroelectricity is a clean and relatively cheap way to produce power, there are sometimes very serious environmental effects when rivers are dammed, such as destroying the natural habitats of wildlife in the area.

31

The Manufacturing Belt

The band of industrial cities that lie around the Great Lakes is part of what is sometimes called the Manufacturing Belt of North America. It has been the most important industrial area of the United States since coal and iron were discovered and started being used in the mid-1800s.

Industry needs steel to make the machinery it uses, and iron and coal are needed to make steel. Huge coal deposits were discovered in the Appalachian Mountains to the south of Lake Erie, and iron ore was found near Lake Superior to the west. The Lakes were the obvious way to transport such bulky and heavy materials, and near the ports where the coal and iron were loaded and unloaded grew the steel industries. Around these industries developed many of the huge industrial cities of North America, such as Chicago and Detroit.

As well as supplying their own region, these cities sell their products throughout the United States and all over the world. Although the Manufacturing Belt is still one of the great industrial areas of the world, it has many problems because it is so old. The cities are overcrowded and polluted and much of the machinery is old-fashioned or out-of-date.

Two hydroelectric stations on the Niagara River; the one on the left supplies people in the United States, the one on the right supplies Canadians.

7. THE ST LAWRENCE SEAWAY

The Soo Locks at Sault Ste Marie between Lake Superior and Lake Huron. A section of the rail bridge has been lifted to allow the cargo ship through.

Canals and locks

For early Europeans the St Lawrence and its tributaries were the only practical means of moving people and goods inland – overland routes were too difficult and dangerous. Along the deep wide river from Montréal to the Atlantic Ocean there are no obstacles, so this stretch has always been a natural waterway for ships of all sizes. However rapids just upstream of Montréal made it impossible to take more than small boats upriver. Canoes 12 m long that could hold a crew of six to twelve men, were about the biggest boats that could make the slow trip upstream to Lake Superior with their cargo.

As ships became larger and trade across the region grew, improvements were made; for example the first canal bypassing the Niagara Falls was opened in 1833. In 1855 the Soo locks and canal were built allowing the first shipments of iron ore from the shores of Lake Superior to the newly-growing industrial areas of the southern lakes. However, still no large ships could travel along the stretch from Montréal to Lake Ontario.

It was not until 1959 that the St Lawrence Seaway was completed. It has become the longest inland navigation system of North America, stretching 3,750 km from Duluth on Lake Superior to the Atlantic Ocean. The Seaway proper starts just upriver of Montréal. To avoid rapids both on the St Lawrence and on the various rivers between the Great Lakes, deep canals and locks had to be built. Other waterways (such as between Lakes Huron and Erie) were dredged to deepen them.

The greatest feat was the building of the modern Welland Canal, the Niagara Falls bypass between Lakes Ontario and Erie. The drop between the lakes is about 100 m, and eight locks were built along the 43 km of canal. The diagram on page 7 gives an idea of what had to be done to make the route possible for large ships.

The diagram on page 7 gives an idea of what had to be done to make the route possible for large ships.

Facts about the St Lawrence Seaway
Length of St Lawrence Seaway from the Atlantic Ocean to Lake Superior: 3,750 km. Locks: 7 locks on St Lawrence River (taking ships up over 70 m), 8 locks on Welland Canal (raising ships nearly 100 m), 1 on Soo Canal. In all 16 locks deal with drop of 177 m. Hydroelectricity: the United States and Canadian governments who built the Seaway also used it as an opportunity to construct several hydroelectric stations along the St Lawrence.

Using the Seaway

Although 30,000-tonne ships can use the Seaway and sail all the way from the Atlantic Ocean to Duluth, the canals were not built wide or deep enough to take the many giant ships that now sail the oceans. Cargo is therefore quite often brought downstream to one of the St Lawrence ports and then transferred to bigger ocean-going ships for its journey across the Atlantic.

The Seaway also has the problem that

The Welland Canal; ships are taken down 100 m through eight locks.

The St Lawrence at Québec, in winter. A channel is kept clear by ice breakers as far as Montréal, but upstream the Seaway is impassable in winter.

it freezes in winter, like most of Canada's waterways. For four or five months of the year (between December and April) the canals and many of the ports along the Seaway are unusable; even ice breakers cannot force a channel. Montréal is the highest point upstream that ocean-going ships can reach in winter, and only because ice breakers work constantly to keep the channel open as far as this. The Gulf of St Lawrence too is difficult to navigate in early summer because thick fogs come down like a blanket.

The ships that use the Great Lakes are called lakers. They are long and narrow and the standard ones (about 220 m long) can use the St Lawrence Seaway to come downriver to Montréal. New larger bulk carriers (ships especially designed to carry large amounts of loose cargo like wheat or coal) have been built to sail the Lakes, but they are unable to use the narrow Welland Canal and so reach the lower part of the St Lawrence Seaway. Although far inland, the Great Lakes are not always plain sailing for ships — terrible storms blow up and fogs come down for days on end.

8. A TRADING ROUTE

The mouth of the St Lawrence River points like an arrow towards Europe across the Atlantic Ocean. Looking at a map of the world (a globe shows it even more clearly) you can see how the St Lawrence, as well as being the most eastern gateway into the North American continent, provides one of the shortest routes to Europe.

Since the arrival of the first Europeans, the St Lawrence has been a great trade route, but the opening of the Seaway made it even more important. Ports on the Great Lakes suddenly became international ports, shipping goods direct to Europe as well as to the big cities of the Canadian heartland. Over 10,000 ships a year sail the St Lawrence carrying millions of tonnes of cargo. Thousands more sail the Great Lakes.

Wheat is stored at this huge grain elevator before being loaded on to a bulk carrier.

Grains and mineral ores

One of the most important goods shipped along this route is wheat from the prairies. From farms, wheat is taken by rail to huge elevators (storage towers) at towns like Duluth and Thunder Bay on Lake Superior. Here the wheat is cleaned and graded before being loaded on to bulk carriers. The wheat is transported across the lakes to American or Canadian cities or down the St Lawrence to export abroad.

Wheat can be shipped directly across the Atlantic to Europe, but most is unloaded and stored at ports (from Montréal downstream) on the St Lawrence. These river ports stay open all year round and so grain can be shipped out from here at any time.

The banks of the St Lawrence near ports such as Baie-Comeau and Montréal are lined with elevators that load grain directly on to ships.

The other two most important cargoes along the Seaway are coal and iron ore. Coal is brought down from the Appalachian coalfields and shipped from ports such as Toledo and Cleveland up and down the Seaway to other steel and manufacturing centres. Iron ore used to be shipped across the Great Lakes to industrial cities in great quantities from mines near Lake Superior, but the ore there has gradually been running out. Now from the opposite direction comes iron ore mined at Schefferville: from the port of Sept-Iles it is shipped upstream via the St Lawrence Seaway to the Great Lakes.

This map shows the main trading routes for commodities along the St Lawrence River.

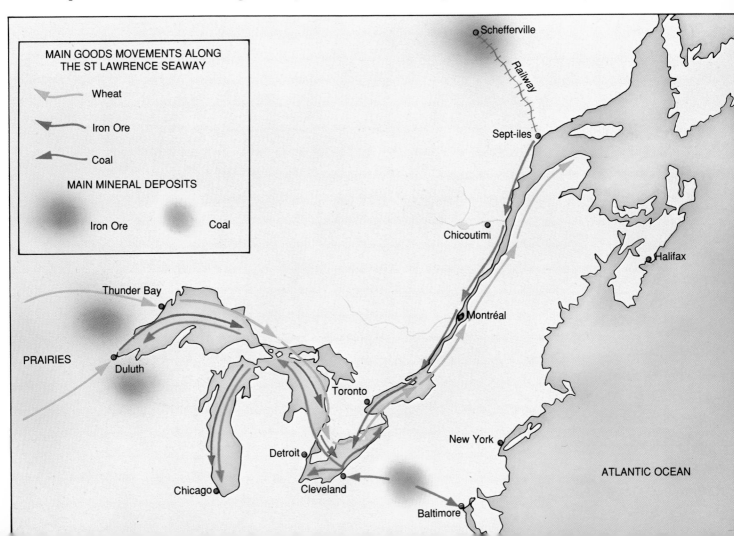

MAIN GOODS MOVEMENTS ALONG THE ST LAWRENCE SEAWAY

Wheat

Iron Ore

Coal

MAIN MINERAL DEPOSITS

Iron Ore   Coal

Schefferville

Railway

Sept-iles

Chicoutimi

Halifax

Thunder Bay

PRAIRIES

Duluth

Montréal

Toronto

Detroit

New York

Chicago

Cleveland

Baltimore

ATLANTIC OCEAN

Huge storage towers at ports on the St Lawrence allow ships to load bulk goods – this ship is loading cement.

The future for the Seaway

The use of ships and the Seaway to transport goods depends on many factors, the most important being the cost of using ships compared to other forms of transport. Generally bulky cargoes (such as grain and ores) can be transported more cheaply by ship than by road or even rail. However, if the ship has no cargo to bring back on its return trip it can lose money. Along the St Lawrence some ships taking down coal or grain are able to make the journey back carrying iron ore from Sept-Iles.

For various reasons the Seaway is not always practical; because it can only take ships up to a certain size, because of ice in winter, because ships have to pay high tolls to use the canals, and because there are delays at bottlenecks like the Welland Canal. Whether the Seaway is used depends too on where the cargo is going: if it is destined for Asia (which is where more and more products are going from North America), then taking goods by rail to the Pacific ports is the better route. Even if it is going to Europe, it may be cheaper to take it by rail direct to an ice-free port like Montréal.

Other factors that affect costs and the way goods like grain are transported, include whether the port through which the cargo passes can handle large ships, and how many times the cargo has to be loaded and unloaded along the way. The price of fuel is also very important – if it rises, rail transport might be cheaper. As well as railways, the St Lawrence Seaway is also competing with routes via the Mississippi River system and the East Coast ports of the United States.

Dan McDonald

'I am the mate on this motor vessel *Patterson*. She is a Great Lakes bulk freighter, 240 m long, carrying cargoes around the Great Lakes and St Lawrence. We transport supplies of grain from Thunder Bay on Lake Superior down to the lower St Lawrence; Montréal or Québec City. Then we pick up iron ore and take it to Chicago. The worst weather we encounter is fog or heavy snowstorms; sailing through the busy waterways is no fun when you can't see anything. It is even more scary than stormy weather on the lakes. When the Seaway freezes up, at the end of December, we lay up the boat. Then I return home to Toronto, and maybe fly off to some sunshine.'

The St Lawrence Seaway is still a major route serving North America but there are other ways to transport goods that might be used more easily and cheaply instead. The Seaway's biggest drawbacks as a trade route are the limited size of ships that it can take and its closure during the winter because of ice. The St Lawrence downstream of Montréal has none of these problems and so is likely to remain an important international shipping route.

A Belgian ship carries a mineral cargo down the Welland Canal on its way to Europe.

9. POLLUTION AND THREATS TO WILDLIFE

Left *Beavers build dams and lodges (homes) of sticks and mud.*

Below *Salmon are the most popular fish caught in the St Lawrence area.*

Wildlife

The St Lawrence River and its tributaries have a huge variety of wildlife. There are something like two hundred types of fish including eel and salmon that swim upriver from the sea into fresh water to spawn. The sea tides and fresh water that flow into the St Lawrence mean that a mixture of seawater and freshwater plants, animals and fish thrive here.

As we saw above, the open sea around the Gulf of St Lawrence is rich in fish: the sea currents in this area are breeding grounds for tiny fish like capelin and these attract larger fish such as cod. Hungry cod follow the shoals of small fish in summer to these waters; in winter the cod migrate south to deeper waters.

One of the most famous creatures of

Whales

As well as the beluga whale, the humpback, the common and the huge blue whale also swim up the St Lawrence to feed on the rich plankton in the river. Whales used to be hunted for their oil which was used for making soap as well as in other industrial processes. At the beginning of the twentieth century there were thought to be about 5,000 belugas that regularly visited the St Lawrence but there are now only about 600 of them left. Below, beluga whales playing in the icy waters of the Gulf of St Lawrence.

the St Lawrence is the beluga whale. Sailors used to call it the 'sea canary' because of the many different noises it makes – from a 'moo' to all sorts of claps and clangs. The beluga is a white whale growing up to five metres long with flippers that it uses to paddle backward and forward. It lives in herds. There are another six species of whale that come up the St Lawrence in summer, sometimes as far up as where it is joined by the Saguenay River. The whales are attracted by the plankton-rich waters.

Wild animals are mostly found in the untouched areas of the Canadian Shield to the north of the river; these include caribou, moose, black bear, raccoon, wolf and beaver. Beavers build dams of small branches, stones and earth across streams to make ponds and often construct dome-shaped 'houses' out of sticks and mud. They eat tender bark and twigs and bury wood at the bottom of the water for food later.

Falling numbers of Atlantic cod have brought hardship to small fishing communities like this one near the mouth of the St Lawrence.

The cold winters of this northern climate mean that wildlife has had to learn to adapt to the cold, hibernate or migrate to a warmer place. Twice a year, the St Lawrence becomes a corridor for migrating birds (some two-thirds of North American birds migrate). This long flyway provides food for the thousands of ducks and geese that fly south in the autumn and north in the spring.

Humans and the environment

Wild creatures in the St Lawrence and Great Lakes region have suffered because of the way humans have used the land and water. Many have lost their habitats and their source of food or have been so disturbed by human activity that they have either moved away or died out. Overhunting has had terrible effects on animal populations too, for example the whale, the beaver and the buffalo of the prairies. For other animals, it has been humans' waste products that have poisoned the water and land.

Industry is one of the main polluters, especially the chemicals that factories pour away and those that seep out from waste dumps. The Great Lakes used to teem with sturgeon, Atlantic salmon, trout and whitefish but now it is mainly coarse fish such as carp and perch. In the waters of the St Lawrence, it is thought that beluga whales and fish have been poisoned by aluminium waste coming down the Saguenay River from the huge aluminium smelters at Chicoutimi-Jonquière.

Although there are controls on what they are allowed to do, it is difficult to make sure that all factories follow these rules. Many of the poisonous substances cannot be seen, smelt or tasted. Even though controls are stricter now, it will take many years to get rid of all the chemicals that were poured into the lakes in the past.

Parts of the Great Lakes/St Lawrence region are heavily populated and industrialized and there is serious pollution.

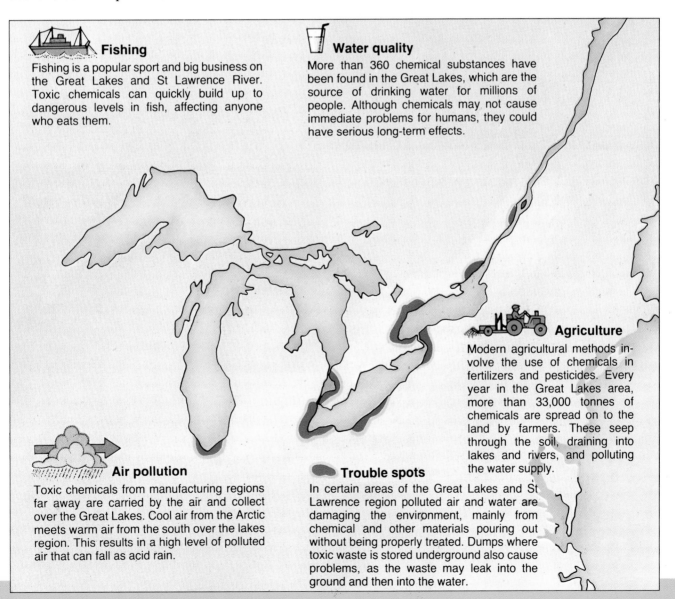

Fishing

Fishing is a popular sport and big business on the Great Lakes and St Lawrence River. Toxic chemicals can quickly build up to dangerous levels in fish, affecting anyone who eats them.

Water quality

More than 360 chemical substances have been found in the Great Lakes, which are the source of drinking water for millions of people. Although chemicals may not cause immediate problems for humans, they could have serious long-term effects.

Agriculture

Modern agricultural methods involve the use of chemicals in fertilizers and pesticides. Every year in the Great Lakes area, more than 33,000 tonnes of chemicals are spread on to the land by farmers. These seep through the soil, draining into lakes and rivers, and polluting the water supply.

Air pollution

Toxic chemicals from manufacturing regions far away are carried by the air and collect over the Great Lakes. Cool air from the Arctic meets warm air from the south over the lakes region. This results in a high level of polluted air that can fall as acid rain.

Trouble spots

In certain areas of the Great Lakes and St Lawrence region polluted air and water are damaging the environment, mainly from chemical and other materials pouring out without being properly treated. Dumps where toxic waste is stored underground also cause problems, as the waste may leak into the ground and then into the water.

Above *Many steel mills lie on the shores of the Great Lakes.*

Right *The Lachine Canal in Montréal.*

AVIS

Le niveau élevé de
pollution des eaux du
canal rend la pratique
du canotage et de la
baignade non sécuritaire.

Environnement Canada
Parcs

NOTICE

Canal waters are considered
unsafe for swimming
and boating due to
high pollution levels.

Environment Canada
Parks

Air pollution affects the area too. Poisonous chemicals are pumped into the air from the industrial areas around the lakes and acid rain is produced. This can kill plants such as trees as well as running into water supplies. In one area in Québec, nine-tenths of the fish species disappeared because the water was so acid. Farming is another serious and growing source of pollution. Millions of tonnes of chemicals are used in modern farming, to fertilize fields and prevent crop diseases. The chemicals gradually work their way into lakes and rivers.

With well over 50 million people living in the area, human waste is also a problem pollutant. At the end of the last century there were typhoid and cholera epidemics in the Great Lakes cities because raw sewage was going into the lakes which were used for drinking water supplies. Since 1925 water from the lakes and river has been treated to

Fishing for salmon in the Thousand Island area. Pollution controls can benefit all who live in or use the river and lakes.

make it safe for humans to use. But humans can still be poisoned from fish (chemicals build up to dangerous levels in fish) and warnings have to be given against eating some species. Because harmful substances are washed away more easily by the flowing water, the St Lawrence does not become as polluted as the lakes; even so, the river had to be closed to eel fishing in 1970. Now all seafood except some shellfish is safe to eat.

Humans suffer in other ways too. The St Lawrence and Great Lakes are recreation areas for the huge population of the region – people sail, fish, swim and sunbathe in summer. Pollution has ruined people's enjoyment of the waters; some of the beaches on the St Lawrence and the Great Lakes are regularly closed to the public because the water is so full of dangerous waste.

The unchecked use of the St Lawrence River and the Great Lakes needs to be thought about for the future, not just for the benefit of wildlife but also for human beings. One way to keep the problems at bay is to keep on spending billions of dollars cleaning up and controlling the harmful substances that are produced. Another way is for humans to change their lifestyles and give up using substances that produce dangerous or unpleasant waste and use farming methods that do not need so many chemicals. Either way there will have to be many changes so that this great natural water resource of North America does not die or become useless for the millions of people that depend on it.

GLOSSARY

Acid rain   Rain that has poisonous substances in it; usually they come from the untreated chemicals in factory smoke.

Aluminium   A lightweight metal.

Buffalo   A kind of wild ox found in North America also called a bison.

Canals   Artificial waterways.

Caribou   A North American reindeer.

Colonies   Countries that have been settled or conquered by another country and which are governed by that country.

Continent   A large land mass.

Crop   Something that is grown and harvested by humans.

Deposited   When something is dropped or left on the land.

Destination   The pre-arranged end of a journey for people or cargoes.

Dredge   To dig out mud and silt from a canal, river or other waterway to deepen it.

Eroded   Worn away by water, ice or wind.

Export   To sell goods to foreign countries.

Fertile   Able to make things grow well.

Glacial silt   Fine soil or ground rock left by slow-moving rivers of ice called glaciers.

Habitats   Natural homes of animals or plants.

Hibernate   To spend the winter in an inactive state resembling sleep.

Hydroelectricity   Electricity made from the power of falling water.

Ice Age   One of several periods in the Earth's history when large parts of the planet were covered in ice.

Immigrants   People who come from one country to settle in another.

Lobster   A shellfish found in the sea or rivers with eight legs, two long claws and a hard shell.

Locks   Sections of a waterway that may be closed off to control the water level and the raising and lowering of boats.

Lumberjacks   People employed to fell trees and organize the transport of the timber.

Midwest   The central region of North America.

Migrating   Moving from one place to settle in another.

Moose   A large North American deer.

Navigable   Describes a waterway that is wide, deep and safe enough for boats.

Nomads   People who do not live in a fixed place but move around.

Ore   The natural material (often rock) from which metals come.

Pelts   The skins of animals with fur, such as beavers.

Peninsula   A narrow strip of land projecting into a sea or lake.

Persecution   Being treated cruelly, often because of religious or political beliefs.

Plankton   Tiny, often invisible creatures that drift or float in the sea.

Province   A district or region that is governed as a unit of the nation.

Pulped   Wood that has been squashed until it becomes soft and mushy. It can then be used to make paper.

Rapids   Sections of a river where the water is churned up by rocks or strong currents.

Reservations   Areas of land set aside for a special purpose, such as a home for native North Americans.

Sewage   Liquid waste from houses and factories.

Silt   Fine particles of soil or sand carried by water.

Smelters   Factories that heat and melt metal ores to obtain the metal.

Spawn   When fish, frogs or shellfish lay their eggs.

Terrain   The physical character of land.

Tolls   Fees charged to vehicles or ships before they can use certain stretches of roads, bridges or waterways.

Tributaries   Smaller rivers that join the main river.

Typhoid and cholera epidemics   Serious outbreaks of the two dangerous diseases, typhoid and cholera.

Upper reaches   The stretch of river furthest away from the sea.

BOOKS TO READ AND FURTHER INFORMATION

As well as the books listed below, look through other books about Canada and the United States. Quite a few will have something about the St Lawrence and Great Lakes area.

Canada – Good neighbour to the World by Adam Bryant (Dillon Press, 1987)
Canada by J Brickenden (Wayland, 1988)
Let's Go to Canada by K Lye (Franklin Watts, 1984)
People and Places: Canada by L Bender (Macmillan, 1988)
World in View, Canada by Jane M Sunday (Heinemann 1992).

For general background for older readers
North America by J H Paterson (OUP 1984)
Canadian Geographical Journal (most issues have something about the St Lawrence or Great Lakes).

Organizations to contact:
There are few organizations based in Britain that have information specifically about the St Lawrence River. However the Québec Government Office have plenty of useful information about the province of Québec, much of which is to do with the river, its surroundings and the people of the area.
Their address is:
Québec Government Office, 59 Pall Mall, London SW1Y 5JH Tel: 071 930 8314.

Picture acknowledgements
All photographs including the cover are by Laurence Fordyce except the following: Robert Estall Photos 6, 11 (lower); Peter Newark's Pictures 12, 13, 14; Oxford Scientific Films/Tony Martin 41; Tony Stone Worldwide/John Edwards 24, 25, Alain Le Garsmeur 35. The map on page 5 is by Peter Bull Design, and artwork on pages 7, 37 and 43 is by John Yates.

INDEX

Numbers in **bold** refer to illustrations